Young Ben Franklin

Young Ben Franklin

by Laurence Santrey
illustrated by John Lawn

Troll Associates

Library of Congress Cataloging in Publication Data

Santrey, Laurence.
    Young Ben Franklin.

    Summary: Focuses on events from Benjamin Franklin's
youth in Boston which proved influential in his later
life.
    1. Franklin, Benjamin, 1706-1790—Childhood and youth
—Juvenile literature.   2. Statesmen—United States—
Biography—Juvenile literature.   [1. Franklin, Benjamin,
1706-1790.   2. Statesmen]   I. Lawn, John, ill.   II. Title.
E302.6.F8S324   973.3′092′4 [B] [92]   81-23067
    ISBN 0-89375-768-3   AACR2
    ISBN 0-89375-769-1 (pbk.)

Young Ben Franklin

Bells chimed in the steeple of the Old South Church. They rang out clearly over colonial Boston. It was a cold, crisp Sunday morning.

Most of the town's twelve thousand citizens were in church. But not the family of Josiah Franklin. They were at home, in their small wooden house on Milk Street. Early this morning—January 17, 1706—a baby boy had been born. Now there was much excitement.

"Papa, what will you name my new brother?" asked seven-year-old Sarah.

Josiah sat back in his chair, puffing on his pipe. After a moment, he said, "We shall call him Benjamin."

Sarah nodded. "That will make Uncle Benjamin very happy."

"Maybe *this* Benjamin will have better sense than our uncle," said James. At nine years old, James was already a very serious person. "What use are his scribblings? Or that silly kind of spelling he invented?"

Josiah frowned at his son. "My brother is a clever man, James. He writes fine poems and useful prose. And he can take down an entire sermon in his shorthand. I would be most pleased if this Benjamin is half so clever as his uncle."

Young Ben Franklin was a very clever boy, indeed. He was curious about everything, asking question after question. With ten older brothers and sisters in the house, there was always someone around to answer him. So it was, that by the time he was four years old, Ben was reading quite well.

Josiah was very proud of his youngest son, especially when friends praised the bright little boy. "He will be a fine scholar," said one man. "Perhaps even another Cotton Mather." This was a great compliment, for Mather was the most highly respected Puritan minister in Boston.

The idea that one of his children was especially bright filled Josiah with joy. He was just a candlemaker. He would never be rich or famous or powerful. But his Benjamin could be all of those things! Why, he would be the first Franklin to go to a real school.

While his father made plans for the future, Ben enjoyed being a little boy. He explored the neighborhood. He watched the tall sailing ships being loaded and unloaded in Boston Harbor. He played with friends on a grassy meadow called the Common. Sometimes he marched around Fort Hill, imitating the red-coated soldiers of the British army. There was much for a young boy to do in the busy colonial town.

When he was six, Ben's family moved from the tiny house on Milk Street to a larger house at the corner of Union and Hanover Streets. By that time, there were two more children in the family, both girls, and that made thirteen Franklin children living at home.

Along with his furniture and the tools of his trade, Josiah moved the symbol of Franklin the Candlemaker—a large blue ball. It was his trademark, one that everyone would know on sight. The blue ball also served as the Franklins' address. Houses didn't have numbers in those days. If you wanted to find someone's home, you looked for the place with four maple trees in front, or the double doors painted green, or something else that made it stand out from the houses around it.

Shops were identified in the same way. The cobbler's shop had a large shoe hanging above the front door. The blacksmith's shop might have a horseshoe above the door. There were hundreds of shops, each with its own sign, in the winding streets of Boston.

It was to one of these, the general store, that Ben hurried one day when he was seven years old. He laughed as he skipped along the dirt street, hearing the copper coins clinking in his pocket. He felt very rich with the pennies he had just gotten as a holiday present.

Tweeet! Tweeeet!

Ben stopped and stared at a boy blowing a shiny red whistle. The boy was standing outside the general store. With each shrill blast Ben's eyes grew wider. What a fine, sharp sound! What a handsome whistle!

Ben brushed past the boy and into the store. There were all kinds of toys for sale. Tops. Games. Dolls. Wooden soldiers. Balls. But Ben saw only one thing—a box filled with shiny red whistles. He picked the one he liked best, gave all his money to the storekeeper, and ran home.

Very pleased with his new toy, Ben went whistling thoughout the house, disturbing the whole family.

"Goodness, what a loud whistle you have," said Ben's mother, with a smile. Abiah Franklin was a kind and patient woman. "What else did you buy?"

"Nothing else," Ben answered. "I spent every penny on this." And he blew another ear-piercing blast.

"You spent all of your money for *that!*" James taunted. "You are a fool."

Ben's brothers and sisters began to laugh. "You could have had four whistles for that price," said Samuel.

17

"Or a whole troop of wooden soldiers," teased Josiah, Jr.

"Or a doll and a ball and a great bag of sweets," sighed Sarah.

Ben's lower lip trembled. He began to cry. He flung the whistle to the floor. There was a fresh burst of laughter.

"Hush, now!" said Abiah Franklin. "You have teased your brother enough. Each of you has chores to do—get to them!"

Ben sat by the fireplace, sobbing quietly. "What a fool I was," he thought. "But I shall not do that again!"

Ben never forgot that day. There would be times when he felt tempted to buy something he really didn't need. Then he would say to himself, "Don't give too much for the whistle."

It was a lesson in many different ways. Ben believed that anyone who tries too hard for friends, fame, or popularity pays too high a price "for the whistle." And he would use this lesson to guide him for the rest of his life.

Young Ben was learning a lot. To the delight of his namesake, Uncle Benjamin, the boy read everything he could put his hands on. He also wrote well for a boy his age. When Josiah Franklin sent a letter to his brother, who lived in London, England, Ben always added a few words of his own. Even before he had one day of schooling, Ben was a star pupil!

When he was eight, Ben entered the Free Grammar School of Boston. He was a quick student. In one year's time he advanced three grades, learning his lessons in Latin and Greek far faster than his classmates.

But at the end of the year, Ben's father took him out of the school. It was clear that young Ben did not want to become a minister. Although he shared his family's faith in God, Ben had little interest in sermons and religious services. "Well, then," Mr. Franklin decided, "I'll not waste time sending the child to this school."

Instead, Ben was enrolled in George Brownwell's "writing school." It was a two-block walk from home, and Ben was glad to go there. He studied penmanship, composition, and spelling. He learned to make a quill pen from a goose feather, how to sharpen it, and how to keep it in good writing condition. He also studied simple addition, subtraction, multiplication, and division—but with poor results. In fact, he failed arithmetic. This made his father feel that Ben was not cut out to be a scholar.

Even though Ben did not do well in arithmetic, it was clear that he was unusually bright and inventive. Ben could outswim any of his friends in races across mile-wide Mill Cove. But he wanted to go even faster. He was sure there had to be a way. He thought about the shape of oars, and how they worked in the water. He thought about the paddles on the mill wheel. He watched ducks glide in the water, pushing with their webbed feet.

He put these facts together and made four
wooden paddles for himself. Then he tied two to
his hands and two to his feet. And to his friends'
amazement—and his own pleasure—the paddles
nearly doubled his speed as a swimmer.

Ben had another idea to make swimming
easier. He used a kite to do it. (All through his
life Ben was fascinated by kites. Years later he
would use one in his famous experiment to
prove that lightning is electricity.)

Ben lay on his back in the water, holding the
string of the kite. When the wind came up, it
carried the kite—and Ben—across Mill Cove.
His friends ran along the shore, cheering him
on.

Another of Ben's schemes was not a big success. In fact, it earned him a scolding. At one edge of Mill Cove there was a salt marsh, where the boys fished for minnows. The only trouble was, they got their clothes soaked when they stood in the marsh. And they were punished when they got home.

One day, Ben noticed a large pile of stones near the marsh. He knew they were for a house that was being built nearby. Only they were *so* perfect for what he had in mind.

"Let's take a few of these stones," Ben said to his friends. "With them we will build a wharf to stand on. No more wet stockings, no more angry parents."

The boys agreed it was a fine plan. When evening came, the men working on the house went home. Now the boys got busy, hauling the stones to the marsh. It took hours of hard work, but at last they had a sturdy wharf to fish from. Then they went home, tired, but very pleased with themselves.

The next morning, the builders discovered many stones were missing. They also discovered the brand-new stone wharf. The boys were soon tracked down and soundly punished for their misdeed. Ben, the ringleader, told the whole story to his father. Then he asked, "Don't you think a stone wharf in the marsh is useful?"

Josiah shook his head. "Think on the great trouble you have given the workers. And the punishment you have brought upon your friends," he said. "I hope you have learned a lesson from this: That which is not honest cannot be truly useful."

It was time, his father felt, for ten-year-old Ben to learn an honest, useful trade. And so, in the small shop on Union Street, he began to teach the boy candlemaking. Ben watched his father chop slabs of sheep and oxen fat into small chunks. These were thrown into a large wooden tub filled with boiling water. As the fat melted, the waste sank to the bottom of the tub. The pure fat, called tallow, floated on top of the water. This hot tallow was poured into metal molds. That is how candles were made in those days.

Ben's job was to cut the twisted cotton threads that were used as candlewicks. He also had to fill the candle molds with tallow. It was hot, smelly work, and Ben hated it.

After two years of this drudgery, Ben told his father, "I will never be a candlemaker. Please let me go to sea."

Josiah refused Ben's request. The Franklins had already lost a son, Josiah, Jr., who went to sea and never returned. Mr. Franklin did not want to lose his youngest son the same way. Still, he did agree that Ben and candlemaking were not right for each other.

Hoping to find the right trade, Mr. Franklin took twelve-year-old Ben on long walks through Boston. They visited many different Leather Apron men, as craftsmen were called in colonial times. They were given this name because they wore thick leather aprons to protect their clothing as they worked.

Ben was fascinated by the skilled artisans as they plied their trades. There were glass cutters, painters, gemsmiths, locksmiths, blacksmiths, nailers, weavers, brewers, bakers, felt makers, pewterers, rope makers, sail makers, masons, brick makers, tile makers, pump makers, glove makers, furriers, cobblers, and many more.

These were the hard-working people who were making Boston a lively and prosperous city. They were also the proud and fearless citizens whose sons would one day fight for their country's independence.

As Ben and his father visited each shop, the young boy learned about the special talents it took to be a true craftsman. There were no machines to make things. Everything had to be made by hand. And to do a good job took time, patience, and great skill.

What Ben learned on those walks around

Boston served him well throughout his life. He learned to use tools of many sorts and to do all kinds of household repairs. Most important, he learned how to turn into reality the many inventions his creative mind dreamed up. The Franklin stove, the lightning rod, astronomical instruments, bifocal eyeglasses, a combination chair and ladder, a clothes-pressing machine, scientific equipment—every one of these, and more, came about because of the education he gained on those walks and visits!

Finally, a decision was made. Ben was apprenticed to his twenty-one-year-old brother, James, who owned a printing shop on Queen Street. First, Ben had to sign "articles of indenture." This was a contract that said Ben would work for James for nine years. That meant he would be twenty-one before he could work anywhere else. Until then, Ben was to work hard and faithfully, six days a week. He had to keep James's trade secrets from all others. He had to be honest, reliable, and obedient.

The contract said what James had to do, too. He was to teach Ben the printing trade and to provide him with food, clothing, and a place to live. James also was to pay Ben a small salary in the last year of his apprenticeship.

The young beginner set the metal type to be printed, ran errands, and swept the shop. He also helped mix the inks, hung the printed sheets to dry, and did any other task James set him to.

Ben worked twelve hours a day. Even so, he found time to educate himself. He read books on grammar, philosophy, science, and logic. Ben taught himself the arithmetic he had not learned in Mr. Brownwell's school.

One day, Ben made a proposal to James. "You are now paying for my meals," Ben said. "If you give me just half of that board money, I will take care to feed myself."

James agreed right away, because this plan would save him money. It was a bargain for Ben, too, since he was a very light eater. His diet cost so little that he was able to save money, which he used for buying books. Ben was always careful with money. As he would later write, "Waste nothing."

Ben also continued to write. His first published work was a poem called *The Lighthouse Tragedy,* about the recent drowning of a lighthouse keeper, his wife, and daughter, in Boston Harbor. As soon as Ben finished writing this poem, James set it in print as a broadside. Broadsides were eighteenth-century, one-page magazines with poems or stories printed on them. Ben then went out into the streets of Boston, selling the broadsides at a penny each.

Because people were still talking about the drownings, the poem sold very well. Ben soon followed this with a poem about the recent capture of the pirate, Blackbeard. This ballad wasn't as popular as Ben's first effort, and he turned his pen to writing prose.

James's printing shop published a weekly newspaper, the *New England Courant*. It was better than most newspapers of that day, which were poorly written and dull. James and several of his friends added some humor along with the lists of ships entering and leaving Boston and the bits of news from other colonies. This light touch came in the form of made-up letters to the editor, signed by Timothy Turnstone, Ichabod Henroost, Abigail Afterwit, Homespun Jack, Tabitha Talkative, and Tom Penshallow.

It seemed to Ben that he could do as well as any of the older writers. So he sat down and wrote a letter to the editor of the *Courant*. In the letter, sixteen-year-old Ben posed as a middle-aged widow living in the country. The widow, Franklin wrote, had many opinions on many subjects and would, in the future, share them with the *Courant*'s readers. Ben signed the letter, "Silence Dogood." He used that false name because he knew that James would never print anything written by a mere apprentice, and also to follow the humorous style used in the other letters to the editor.

Late at night, when the shop was empty, Ben slipped the Widow Dogood's letter under the front door. James read it in the morning, suspected nothing, and was delighted by its content and writing style. He showed it to his friends. They shared his enjoyment and urged him to print it. And so, on April 2, 1722, Silence Dogood appeared in print for the first time.

There were fourteen letters in all, commenting on poetry, urging education for women, and giving opinions on all sorts of subjects.

The readers loved Silence Dogood's letters. The *Courant* sold better than ever. This made James very happy. But he stopped smiling when it became known that the Widow Dogood was none other than his clever young brother, Ben. And when all of James's friends began paying attention to the teenage apprentice, James became very angry.

There were five years left on the contract between the brothers. Ben wished there was some way to tear up the papers of indenture. But that was not possible. The law was very hard on runaway apprentices. Then something happened. The *Courant* printed some articles insulting the colonial government in Massachusetts. James was arrested and thrown into prison.

Ben ran the newspaper while James was imprisoned for a month. Then James was released, but it wasn't long before he was in trouble again. This time he was forbidden to publish a newspaper. Some friends suggested a way to get around this problem. "Tear up Ben's articles of indenture," said one, "and make him the publisher."

James did not like the idea of giving the *Courant* to his "sassy" younger brother. But there was a warrant out for James's arrest; he had to flee Boston, and he didn't want to see his newspaper stop publishing.

"In time, the warrant will be withdrawn, and you can return," another friend told James. "While you are away, Ben can keep the *Courant* alive for you."

James gave in and tore up Ben's indenture papers. Then he signed the *Courant* over to the teenager. In secret, however, a new set of indenture papers were drawn up. But Ben knew they could never be made public.

Ben was the editor and publisher of the paper (and Silence Dogood, too) for the next eight months. And, under Ben, the newspaper was more successful than ever. Then James came back and wanted things to be the way they were before his arrest. Ben objected, and the brothers quarreled.

"You are still my apprentice," James snarled. "I have the papers that say so."

Ben laughed. "To whom can you show those papers?" he asked. "Be reasonable. You wish the *Courant* to continue, so you use my name as publisher. But since an apprentice may not own a newspaper, our secret must be kept."

James knew Ben was right. If he tried to hold Ben to the agreement, he would lose the newspaper. This angered him even more. From that day on, the brothers fought constantly.

At last, Ben could stand it no longer. He told James he was leaving the printing shop. James immediately asked the other printers in Boston not to hire the young man, and they agreed.

Now there was no way for Ben to earn a living in Boston. So he went to a local bookstore and sold most of his books. With the money he made, Ben bought passage aboard a ship bound for New York. From New York he would travel to Philadelphia, a thriving town in the colony of Pennsylvania. It was September 1723, the beginning of a new life for Benjamin Franklin.

In the years to come, Ben would win fame as the leading printer in Philadelphia and in all the colonies. He would write *Poor Richard's Almanack,* many important scientific papers, and his autobiography. He would found the first lending library and the first fire department. He would create hundreds of inventions and help to establish the University of Pennsylvania.

Even more important, Ben would play a part in his country's fight for independence. Only Ben Franklin signed the American colonies' four most important documents: the Declaration of Independence, the alliance treaty with France, the peace treaty with England, and the United States Constitution. Then, in his later years, he served with distinction as the American ambassador to France.

A most distinguished citizen of the world, Benjamin Franklin died on April 17, 1790, at the age of 84.